EXPLORE M.

Travel Guide

The Citi-scaper

Table of Contents

Introduction

As you approach Madeira, a speck in the vast expanse of the Atlantic, you will feel a sense of wonder and excitement. The island's rugged coastline rises dramatically from the waves, with cliffs plunging into the sea and rocky outcroppings jutting up from the water. This is a place of raw beauty, where nature's power is on full display.

But Madeira is not just a natural wonderland. It is also a cultural and historical treasure trove, with a rich and diverse heritage that spans centuries. From the colorful and bustling markets of Funchal to the ancient churches and fortresses of the island's interior, Madeira is a place that invites exploration and discovery.

As you step off the plane and take your first breath of Madeiran air, you will be struck by the warmth and hospitality of the island's people. Madeirans are known for their friendliness and generosity, and they are eager to share their island with visitors.

Whether you are here for a leisurely holiday or an adrenaline-fueled adventure, Madeira has something to offer. Hike through lush forests and along vertiginous ridges, swim in crystal-clear waters, or simply relax on one of the island's many beaches. Sample the local cuisine, which combines African, Portuguese, and Mediterranean flavors in delicious and unexpected ways, and sip the famous Madeira wine, which has been prized by connoisseurs for centuries.

In this guide, we will take you on a journey through Madeira's many wonders, from its stunning natural landscapes to its vibrant cultural scene. We will introduce you to the island's history, its people, and its traditions, and we will help you plan your perfect Madeiran adventure.

Chapter 1

Overview

Madeira, a Portuguese archipelago located in the Atlantic Ocean, is a breathtakingly beautiful and diverse destination that attracts visitors from around the world. Known as the "Island of Eternal Spring," Madeira boasts a subtropical climate with warm temperatures all year round, making it the perfect place to escape to for those seeking a relaxing and rejuvenating vacation.

Madeira is made up of four main islands: Madeira, Desertas, Porto Santo, and Selvagens. The largest of these islands, Madeira, is where the majority of the population resides, and where most visitors to the archipelago will spend their time. The island is approximately 57 km long and 22 km wide, with a total area of 741km². It is a mountainous island with stunning landscapes, including lush forests, towering peaks, and dramatic cliffs that drop into the ocean.

Visitors to Madeira can enjoy a wide range of outdoor activities, from hiking along the levadas (irrigation channels) that crisscross the island, to swimming in the crystal-clear waters off its many beaches. Madeira is also a haven for wildlife, with numerous species of birds, reptiles, and marine life calling the archipelago home.

One of the most iconic attractions in Madeira is the Funchal Old Town, a charming district filled with cobblestone streets, historic buildings, and quaint cafes. Visitors can explore the town's many museums, art galleries, and markets, or simply soak up the atmosphere while sipping a cup of traditional Madeiran poncha or bica coffee.

Another popular attraction is the Monte Palace Tropical Garden, a stunning botanical garden that covers an area of 70,000m² and is home to over 100,000 different plant species. The garden also features a collection of exotic birds, a museum, and a cafe with panoramic views of the city.

For those seeking a more active holiday, Madeira also offers a range of adventure sports, including canyoning, mountain biking, and paragliding. The island's rugged terrain and stunning vistas make it the perfect destination for outdoor enthusiasts.

Madeira is also famous for its cuisine, which is a blend of Portuguese, African, and Brazilian influences. Visitors can sample traditional dishes such as espetada (grilled skewered beef) and bolo do caco (a type of bread), as well as enjoy the local wines, including the famous Madeira wine.

Overall, Madeira is a unique and unforgettable destination that offers something for everyone. Its stunning natural beauty, rich cultural heritage, and warm and welcoming people make it a must-visit location for any traveler seeking an authentic and enriching experience.

Geography

Geographically, Madeira is part of the Macaronesia region, which includes the Canary Islands, the Azores, Cape Verde, and the Savage Islands. It is the largest island in the Madeira Archipelago, which also includes the smaller islands of Desertas, Porto Santo, and Selvagens.

The island is of volcanic origin, and its rugged terrain is dominated by steep mountains, deep valleys, and cliffs that drop into the ocean. The highest peak on the island is Pico Ruivo, which stands at 1,862 meters (6,109 feet) above sea level. The island is also home to several other peaks over 1,500 meters (4,921 feet), including Pico do Arieiro and Pico das Torres.

Madeira's volcanic origins are evident in its geology, which includes basaltic rocks, lava flows, and volcanic ash deposits. The island's soil is rich in nutrients, which has allowed for the growth of lush vegetation, including subtropical forests, exotic flowers, and fruits such as bananas, mangoes, and avocados.

The island is also home to several rivers, including the Ribeira da Janela, Ribeira Brava, and Ribeiro Frio, which flow through the mountainous terrain, creating breathtaking waterfalls and natural swimming pools.

Madeira has a subtropical climate, with mild temperatures throughout the year. The island experiences high humidity, especially in the coastal areas, and is known for its frequent rain showers. The rain and humidity, combined with the island's volcanic soil, have created a unique environment that is ideal for the growth of flora and fauna.

Madeira is home to several endemic species of plants and animals, including the Madeira laurel forest, which is a UNESCO World Heritage Site. The forest is home to several rare and endangered species, such as the Madeira firecrest, the Madeiran long-toed pigeon, and the Madeira pipistrelle.

In addition to its natural beauty, Madeira has a rich cultural history that is evident in its architecture, museums, and festivals. The island's capital city, Funchal, is a vibrant and bustling city that boasts a historic center with cobblestone streets, colorful buildings, and a beautiful harbor. Visitors can explore museums, art galleries, and churches that showcase the island's cultural heritage.

In conclusion, Madeira is a unique and beautiful island that offers visitors a wide range of natural and cultural experiences. Its rugged terrain, volcanic origins, and subtropical climate have created a diverse and thriving ecosystem that is home to several rare and endangered species. Whether you're interested in hiking, swimming, or exploring the island's cultural heritage, Madeira is a destination that is sure to delight and inspire.

Best Time to Visit

When planning a trip to Madeira, it's important to consider the best time to visit. Madeira is a year-round destination with a subtropical climate that offers pleasant temperatures and plenty of sunshine. However, there are a few factors that can make one time of year better than another for different activities and interests.

The high season for tourism in Madeira is typically from June to August, when the weather is warmest and driest. During this time, the island can be quite busy, and prices for accommodation and activities can be higher. However, if you're looking for a lively atmosphere and lots of events and festivals, this could be the perfect time to visit.

If you prefer to avoid the crowds, consider visiting during the shoulder seasons of spring (March to May) or autumn (September to November). During these months, the weather is still pleasant, and the crowds are thinner, making it a great time to explore the island's natural beauty and cultural attractions.

Winter (December to February) can be a good time to visit for those who enjoy cooler temperatures and quieter surroundings. The weather is mild, with daytime temperatures ranging from 16 to 20 degrees Celsius, and there are fewer tourists around. This time of year is also ideal for whale and dolphin watching, as well as hiking.

Regardless of the time of year, it's important to keep in mind that Madeira is an island with microclimates. This means that while one part of the island may be experiencing sunshine and warmth, another part could be cloudy or rainy. It's always a good idea to check the weather forecast and pack accordingly, especially if you plan to do outdoor activities.

The best time to visit Madeira depends on your interests and preferences. Whether you're looking for a bustling atmosphere or a quiet escape, there's a time of year that's perfect for you. By considering the weather, crowds, and activities you want to do, you can plan a trip to Madeira that's unforgettable.

Visa Requirements

As a Portuguese territory, Madeira follows the visa policy of the Schengen Area. This means that visitors from certain countries need to get a Schengen visa in order to enter the island. However, citizens of many countries are allowed to enter Madeira for short stays without a visa. Here's what you need to know about visa requirements for Madeira:

Do I need a visa to visit Madeira?

If you are a citizen of a country in the European Union (EU), the European Economic Area (EEA), or Switzerland, you do not need a visa to enter Madeira. This includes countries such as France, Germany, Spain, and the United Kingdom. Citizens of some non-EU countries, such as Iceland, Norway, and Liechtenstein, also do not need a visa.

What if I am not a citizen of the EU, EEA, or Switzerland?

If you are not a citizen of any of these countries, you may need a Schengen visa to enter Madeira. The list of countries whose citizens need a visa is subject to change, so it's important to check the latest information from the Portuguese embassy or consulate in your country. Generally speaking, citizens of certain countries e,g. The United States, Australia, Canada, and Japan need a visa to enter Madeira.

What if I am transiting through Madeira?

If you are transiting through Madeira on your way to another destination, you may not need a visa. This depends on your nationality and the length of your layover. Check with your airline and the Portuguese embassy or consulate in your country to determine whether you need a visa for transit through Madeira.

What if I overstay my visa in Madeira?

If you overstay your visa in Madeira, you may be subject to fines or other penalties. You may also be barred from entering the Schengen Area in the future. To avoid any problems, be sure to leave Madeira and the Schengen Area before your visa expires.

Visa requirements for Madeira depend on your nationality. Citizens of the EU, EEA, and Switzerland do not need a visa, while citizens of other countries may need a Schengen visa. If you need a visa, you should apply through the Portuguese embassy in your country. Be sure to check the latest information and requirements before you travel.

Currency

Currency is an important aspect to consider when planning a trip to Madeira. The official currency used on the island is the Euro, which is the same currency used throughout Portugal. It's always a good idea to exchange your currency for Euros before arriving in Madeira, or you can easily exchange your currency at a local bank or currency exchange office on the island.

Most businesses on the island accept credit and debit cards, but it's also a good idea to carry some cash with you, especially when visiting smaller villages or markets. ATMs are readily available throughout Madeira, so you can withdraw Euros as needed.

When it comes to tipping, it's not necessary in Madeira, but it's always appreciated for exceptional service. If you choose to tip, a small amount of 5-10% is appropriate.

It's important to note that Madeira is a relatively affordable destination compared to other European destinations, so your money will go a long way. However, it's always a good idea to plan a budget and stick to it to ensure you have a comfortable and enjoyable trip.

If you're planning on traveling to Madeira from outside the European Union, you may be subject to customs regulations and taxes. It's always a good idea to check with your home country's customs agency to ensure you're aware of any potential fees or restrictions.

The Euro is the official currency in Madeira, credit and debit cards are widely accepted, ATMs are readily available, tipping is not necessary but appreciated, and it's always a good idea to plan a budget and be aware of any potential customs regulations or taxes. By keeping these tips in mind, you'll be well-prepared to enjoy all that Madeira has to offer without any financial worries.

Language and Communication

For travelers visiting Madeira, it is important to be aware of the language and communication practices on the island. Madeira is an autonomous region of Portugal, which means that the official language is Portuguese. However, English is widely spoken and understood in the main tourist areas, particularly by those who work in the hospitality industry.

It is recommended that visitors learn some basic Portuguese phrases to make their stay more enjoyable and to connect with locals on a deeper level. Basic greetings like "Bom dia" (good morning), "Boa tarde" (good afternoon), and "Boa noite" (good evening) can go a long way in building rapport and showing respect for the local culture. "Por favor" (please) and "obrigado" (thank you) are also essential phrases to know.

While English is widely spoken, it is important to keep in mind that some locals may not be fluent. It is always appreciated when visitors make an effort to communicate in Portuguese, even if it is just a few basic phrases.

In addition to spoken language, there are other ways of communicating in Madeira that visitors should be aware of. For example, it is common to use hand gestures to communicate in Portuguese culture. For instance, holding up your index finger and thumb to form a circle means "okay" or "all right," while tapping your wrist with your index finger means "hurry up" or "time is running out."

Visitors should also be aware that Madeiran Portuguese is slightly different from standard Portuguese, with some unique words and phrases. For example, "escadinhas" means "staircase," while "poiso" means "rest stop."

In terms of communication technology, Madeira has a reliable mobile network, and most visitors will be able to use their phones as they would at home. Additionally, there are many Wi-Fi hotspots throughout the island, including in hotels, restaurants, and cafes.

Overall, while English is widely spoken in Madeira, learning some basic Portuguese phrases can greatly enhance a visitor's experience and help them connect with locals on a deeper level. Additionally, understanding the unique communication practices of the region, such as hand gestures and local vocabulary, can also help visitors feel more at home during their stay.

Common phrases

Here are some common phrases that visitors to Madeira might find useful during their stay:

Bom dia - Good morning

Boa tarde - Good afternoon

Boa noite - Good evening

Olá - Hello

Adeus - Goodbye

Por favor - Please

Obrigado (if you're male) or obrigada (if you're female) - Thank you

De nada - You're welcome

Desculpe - Excuse me

Com licença - Pardon me

Sim - Yes

Não - No

Fala inglês? - Do you speak English?

Eu não falo português - I don't speak Portuguese

Eu gostaria de... - I would like to...

Quanto custa? - How much does it cost?

Onde fica...? - Where is...?

À direita - To the right

À esquerda - To the left

Em frente - Straight ahead

Learning these basic phrases can help visitors to communicate with locals and make their stay in Madeira more enjoyable.

Chapter 2

Transportation Options

Transportation in Madeira is an important part of the island's economy and culture. In recent years, the island has seen a great deal of development in its transportation infrastructure and services, allowing for easier ways to get around the island. From the efficient public transportation network to the reliable ferry services, there are plenty of options for getting around Madeira. In addition, Madeira is home to a number of car hire companies, making it possible for visitors to explore the island independently. This guide will provide an overview of the transportation options available in Madeira, as well as some helpful tips for getting around the island.

Getting There

Getting to Madeira is an adventure in itself, with multiple options available for visitors to choose from. Whether you are arriving from Europe, the Americas, or elsewhere in the world, there are several ways to reach this beautiful island paradise.

By Air: The easiest way to get to Madeira is by air, as it is serviced by the Madeira International Airport (Funchal Airport), which is located on the eastern side of the island, just outside the capital city of Funchal. Several airlines operate regular flights to Madeira from major European cities like London, Frankfurt, Paris, and Lisbon, as well as from other international destinations like New York, Toronto, and Dubai. The airport is also well connected to other Portuguese cities like Porto and Lisbon, making it easy to plan a multi-city itinerary.

By Sea: For those who prefer to travel by sea, there are several cruise ships that stop at Madeira on their itinerary, making it a popular destination for luxury cruises in the Atlantic Ocean. The port of Funchal is well-equipped to handle large cruise ships, and visitors can enjoy a comfortable and scenic journey across the ocean to reach Madeira.

By Land: While it is not possible to drive to Madeira, visitors can still arrive by land via the mainland of Portugal, which is connected to Madeira by regular ferry services. The journey takes around 24 hours, and the ferry operates weekly services from Portimao, Algarve and Port of Setubal.

Once you arrive in Madeira, getting around the island is relatively easy. There are several car rental agencies available at the airport, or you can use public transportation like buses and taxis to explore the island. Madeira's roads are well-maintained and easy to navigate, making it a great destination for a road trip.

Madeira is easily accessible by air, sea, or land, making it a popular destination for visitors from all over the world. With so many travel options available, getting to this stunning island paradise is an adventure in itself.

Getting Around

Getting around Madeira is relatively easy, with several transportation options available for visitors to choose from. Whether you prefer to explore the island on your own or with a guided tour, there are plenty of options to suit your travel style and budget.

By Car: Renting a car is a popular way to explore Madeira, as it offers visitors the freedom to travel at their own pace and explore the island's hidden gems. There are several car rental agencies available at the airport, or you can arrange to rent a car from your hotel or a local rental company. Madeira's roads are well-maintained and easy to navigate, making it a great destination for a road trip.

By Bus: Madeira's public transportation system is reliable and affordable, with regular bus services operating throughout the island. The bus network covers most of the major towns and tourist attractions, and the fares are reasonable. You can purchase tickets from the driver or from a ticket machine at the bus station. The buses are comfortable and air-conditioned, making them a great option for those who want to explore the island without driving.

By Taxi: Taxis are readily available in Madeira, and they offer a convenient and comfortable way to get around the island. Taxis operate on a metered fare system, and the rates are reasonable. You can hail a taxi on the street or ask your hotel or restaurant to arrange one for you. Taxis are also a great option for people who want to explore the island but don't want to drive.

By Guided Tour: If you prefer to explore Madeira with a guide, there are several guided tour options available. You can choose from a variety of tours, including sightseeing tours, hiking tours, and wine tours, among others. Guided tours offer visitors the opportunity to learn more about the island's culture, history, and natural beauty, and they are a great way to meet other travelers and make new friends.

Getting around Madeira is very easy and convenient, there are several transportation options available for visitors to choose from. Whether you prefer to explore the island on your own or with a guided tour, there are plenty of options to suit your travel style and budget.

Chapter 3

Accommodation Options

Accommodation in Madeira is varied and plentiful. From basic hostels to luxury resorts, there is something for everyone. Whether you're looking for a beachfront villa or a cozy mountain retreat, Madeira has the perfect place for you to stay. With its stunning vistas, warm climate and vibrant culture, there is no better place to stay than in this beautiful Portuguese archipelago. This guide will provide an overview of the different types of accommodation available in Madeira as well as practical advice for finding the best deal.

Types of Accommodation

When it comes to finding accommodation on the beautiful island of Madeira, visitors will be spoilt for choice. From luxurious hotels to charming guesthouses, there is something to suit every taste and budget. Here are some of the different types of accommodation options available to travelers:

Hotels: Madeira has a wide range of hotels, from luxurious 5-star resorts to more budget-friendly options. Many of the island's hotels offer stunning views of the ocean, and are equipped with top-notch amenities such as spas, swimming pools, and on-site restaurants. Some of the most popular hotels in Madeira include the Belmond Reid's Palace, Pestana Carlton Madeira, and the Savoy Palace.

Guesthouses: For travelers looking for a more intimate and homely atmosphere, guesthouses can be a great option. These smaller, family-run establishments offer comfortable rooms, personalized service, and a chance to experience local culture. Many guesthouses in Madeira are located in historic buildings, adding to the charm and character of the accommodation. Some popular guesthouses on the island include Quinta Jardins do Lago, Casa Velha do Palheiro, and Quinta da Casa Branca.

Villas: If you're traveling with a large group or simply prefer a more private accommodation option, renting a villa can be an excellent choice. Many villas in Madeira come equipped with private pools, gardens, and stunning views. They offer a great way to relax and unwind in privacy, while still being within easy reach of the island's attractions. Some of the most popular villa rental companies on the island include Villa Retreats, Madeira Island Direct, and Madeira Luxury Villas.

Apartments: Apartments are a great option for travelers who prefer more space and the ability to cook their own meals. There is a wide variety of apartments available in

Madeira, from budget-friendly studios to luxurious penthouses. Many apartments offer stunning views of the ocean or the island's lush greenery. Some popular apartment complexes include The Vine, Monumental Palace, and Funchal Design Hotel.

Hostels: For budget-conscious travelers, hostels are a popular accommodation option. Madeira's hostels offer both dormitory-style accommodation and private rooms at affordable prices. They can be a great way to meet other travelers and experience the local culture. Some of the most popular hostels on the island include the Madeira Happy Hostel, Santa Maria Hostel, and the 29 Madeira Hostel.

Camping: Madeira offers several campgrounds for those who prefer a more rustic accommodation option. This can be a great way to immerse yourself in nature and enjoy the island's stunning scenery. Camping is also a relatively inexpensive way to travel, as campsites often offer basic amenities such as showers and toilets. Some popular campsites on the island include Parque de Campismo da Madeira and Camping Porto Moniz.

Rural Tourism: For those looking to get away from the hustle and bustle of the city, rural tourism offers a chance to experience the island's countryside. Visitors can stay in traditional houses and cottages, enjoy homemade meals, and participate in local activities such as hiking and farming. This can be a great way to experience the local culture and way of life. Some popular rural tourism options on the island include Quinta das Vinhas and Quinta do Lombo.

When choosing your accommodation in Madeira, it's important to consider your budget, travel style, and the type of experience you want to have. With so many options available, you're sure to find the perfect accommodation to suit your needs and preferences.

Best Areas to Stay

When visiting Madeira, there are several areas that are popular among visitors for their convenience, accessibility, and variety of accommodation options. Here are some of the best areas to stay in Madeira:

Funchal: As the capital of Madeira, Funchal is the most popular area for visitors to stay. It offers a wide range of accommodation options, from luxurious resorts to budget-friendly guesthouses and hostels. Funchal is also home to many of the island's top attractions, such as the Funchal Cathedral, the Botanical Garden, and the Madeira Wine Museum. The city also boasts a beautiful promenade lined with restaurants, cafes, and shops, making it a great base for exploring the island.

Caniço: Located just a short drive from Funchal, Caniço is a popular area for visitors looking for a quieter, more peaceful stay. It offers a range of accommodation options, including hotels, villas, and apartments, many of which offer stunning views of the ocean. Caniço is also home to several beautiful beaches and hiking trails, making it a great choice for those who love the outdoors.

Porto Santo: If you're looking for a true island getaway, Porto Santo is the place to be. Located just a short ferry ride from Madeira, Porto Santo is a small, quiet island known for its beautiful beaches and crystal-clear waters. It offers a range of accommodation options, including hotels, villas, and apartments, as well as plenty of opportunities for outdoor activities such as hiking, diving, and horseback riding.

Calheta: Located on the west coast of Madeira, Calheta is a popular area for visitors who want to explore the island's natural beauty. It offers a range of accommodation options, including hotels, villas, and apartments, many of which are located near the beach or in the hills overlooking the ocean. Calheta is also home to several hiking trails and is a great base for exploring the island's famous levadas.

Santana: If you're looking for a more rural experience, Santana is a great choice. Located in the north of Madeira, it is known for its traditional thatched-roof houses and beautiful scenery. Visitors can stay in rural tourism accommodations such as guesthouses and cottages, and enjoy activities such as hiking, horseback riding, and visiting local farms.

Ultimately, the best area to stay in Madeira depends on your individual preferences and travel style. With a variety of options available, you're sure to find the perfect base for exploring this beautiful island.

Best Hotels in Madeira

Madeira, a beautiful Portuguese island located in the Atlantic Ocean, is a popular tourist destination due to its stunning natural beauty, mild climate, and rich history. It is also home to some of the best hotels in the world, offering guests unparalleled luxury and comfort during their stay. Here are some of the top hotels in Madeira:

Belmond Reid's Palace: This iconic hotel, built in the 19th century, is a symbol of luxury and sophistication. Located on a cliff overlooking the Atlantic Ocean, it offers stunning views of the sea and surrounding landscapes. The hotel's elegant rooms and suites are decorated in a classic style, with antique furnishings and luxurious fabrics. Guests can indulge in the hotel's world-class spa, swim in the heated outdoor pool, or enjoy a meal at one of its award-winning restaurants.

The Cliff Bay: This elegant hotel, located in Funchal, offers breathtaking views of the Atlantic Ocean and surrounding landscapes. The hotel's rooms and suites are spacious and modern, with private balconies that offer panoramic views of the sea. Guests can enjoy a range of activities, from swimming in the infinity pool to exploring the hotel's lush gardens. The hotel's two restaurants offer exquisite cuisine, while the spa offers a range of treatments and therapies.

Quinta da Casa Branca: This boutique hotel, located in a peaceful corner of Funchal, is surrounded by lush gardens and subtropical vegetation. The hotel's rooms and suites are spacious and stylishly decorated, with private balconies that overlook the gardens or the sea. Guests can relax by the outdoor pool, take a stroll through the gardens, or indulge in a spa treatment. The hotel's restaurant offers a range of local and international dishes, made with fresh, locally sourced ingredients.

Savoy Palace: This luxurious hotel, located in the heart of Funchal, offers guests a modern and sophisticated experience. The hotel's rooms and suites are spacious and elegantly decorated, with private balconies that offer views of the city or the sea. Guests can relax by the hotel's outdoor pool, enjoy a meal at one of its several restaurants, or indulge in a spa treatment. The hotel also has a rooftop bar with panoramic views of Funchal.

Belmond Reid's Palace Villa Cipriani: This luxurious villa, located in the grounds of the Belmond Reid's Palace, offers guests a private and exclusive experience. The villa's rooms and suites are elegantly decorated, with private balconies that offer breathtaking views of the sea. Guests can enjoy the villa's private outdoor pool, gardens, and terrace, or take advantage of the amenities offered by the nearby hotel, including its spa, restaurants, and outdoor pool.

Madeira offers some of the best hotels in the world, each offering guests a unique and luxurious experience. Whether you're looking for stunning views of the sea, lush gardens, or a modern and sophisticated atmosphere, Madeira has a hotel that will meet your needs.

Chapter 4

Culture and History

Madeira, an archipelago located in the Atlantic Ocean, has a rich and fascinating history that is deeply intertwined with its unique culture. The island's history dates back to the 15th century, when Portuguese navigators first discovered and settled on the island. Over the centuries, Madeira has been home to diverse cultures, including Portuguese, African, and European influences, which have all contributed to the development of its distinct identity.

Today, Madeira's culture and history continue to be celebrated and preserved through its traditions, festivals, architecture, and cuisine. In this chapter, we will explore the rich cultural and historical heritage of Madeira, providing a comprehensive overview of its fascinating past and vibrant present.

Museu de Arte Sacra do Funchal

The Museu de Arte Sacra do Funchal, also known as the Museum of Sacred Art, is a must-visit destination for visitors to Madeira who are interested in exploring the rich cultural and religious heritage of the island. Located in the heart of Funchal, the capital city of Madeira, the museum is housed in the beautiful 17th-century Episcopal Palace, which is a fine example of Baroque architecture.

Upon entering the museum, visitors are immediately struck by the impressive collection of religious art and artifacts that are on display. The museum boasts an extensive collection of paintings, sculptures, liturgical vestments, and other objects that span the centuries from the 15th to the 19th. The collection is particularly strong in works of the Flemish and Portuguese schools, with many pieces by well-known artists such as Francisco Henriques, Gregório Lopes, and Josefa d'Óbidos.

One of the highlights of the museum is the impressive collection of silverware, which includes numerous pieces of intricate liturgical vessels, monstrances, and chalices. These pieces are not only visually stunning but also provide a fascinating insight into the religious practices of the island's past.

Another standout feature of the museum is the beautiful chapel, which is located on the ground floor of the palace. The chapel is a fine example of the Baroque style and is adorned with exquisite paintings and sculptures, including a striking altarpiece that dominates the room.

Visitors can also explore the various rooms of the palace, which have been restored to their former glory and provide a fascinating insight into the lives of the bishops who once lived there. The rooms are furnished with beautiful antiques and offer a glimpse into the luxurious lifestyle enjoyed by the island's elite in centuries past.

In addition to the permanent collection, the museum also hosts regular temporary exhibitions, which showcase works by local and international artists. These exhibitions provide a contemporary counterpoint to the museum's historical collections and offer visitors a chance to engage with the vibrant art scene on the island.

Overall, the Museu de Arte Sacra do Funchal is a great destination for any traveler to Madeira who is interested in exploring the island's rich cultural and religious heritage. The museum's impressive collection of art and artifacts, beautiful chapel, and restored palace rooms combine to provide a fascinating and immersive experience that will leave a lasting impression on visitors.

Sé Cathedral

Sé Cathedral, also known as Funchal Cathedral, is a magnificent religious building that is a must-visit for anyone traveling to Madeira. The cathedral, located in the heart of Funchal, is an architectural masterpiece that blends Gothic and Romanesque styles. It is the most prominent landmark of the city and a symbol of Madeira's rich history and culture.

The construction of the cathedral began in 1493 and was completed in the 16th century. The building underwent several renovations and additions over the centuries, which is evident in its architectural style. The facade of the cathedral is made of basalt and white limestone and features a beautiful rose window, which is a highlight of the building.

The interior of the cathedral is just as breathtaking as the exterior. The nave is lined with intricate carvings and gilded decorations, while the vaulted ceiling features ornate paintings. One of the most impressive features of the interior is the high altar, which is made of silver and has a beautiful crucifixion scene at its center.

Visitors can also marvel at the beautiful stained glass windows that date back to the 16th century. These windows are not only beautiful but also tell stories of Madeira's rich religious history. Another interesting feature of the cathedral is the beautiful choir stalls, which are intricately carved and date back to the 16th century.

One of the most unique features of the Sé Cathedral is the Museum of Sacred Art, which is located within the cathedral complex. The museum houses a stunning collection of religious artifacts, including paintings, sculptures, and other works of art. Visitors can explore the museum to learn more about Madeira's religious history and admire the intricate details of these precious artifacts.

The Sé Cathedral is also a popular destination for religious pilgrims. The cathedral is home to the tomb of the island's first bishop, who was canonized by the Catholic Church. Many visitors come to the cathedral to pay their respects and seek solace in this holy place.

If you plan to visit the Sé Cathedral, make sure to schedule enough time to explore both the cathedral and the museum. The cathedral is open to visitors every day, and there is a small admission fee. Guided tours are also available, which can provide more insight into the history and significance of this beautiful landmark.

The Sé Cathedral is a must-visit destination for people traveling to Madeira. With its stunning architecture, beautiful decorations, and rich history, the cathedral is a unique and unforgettable experience that you won't want to miss.

Madeira Story Centre

The Madeira Story Centre is a fascinating museum located in the heart of Funchal, Madeira. The museum is dedicated to telling the story of Madeira, from its geological formation to its cultural and historical development.

The museum uses state-of-the-art technology to create an interactive and immersive experience for visitors. It is divided into several themed sections, each with its own exhibits and displays. Visitors can start their journey through the museum by watching a short film about Madeira's creation and evolution.

One of the most interesting exhibits in the museum is the interactive volcanic eruption display. This exhibit uses special effects to simulate a volcanic eruption, allowing visitors to experience the power and destructive force of nature firsthand.

Another popular exhibit is the section on Madeira's history and culture. Here, visitors can learn about the island's discovery by Portuguese explorers, the development of its economy, and the evolution of its cultural traditions. The exhibit features many artifacts, including traditional costumes, handicrafts, and musical instruments.

The Madeira Story Centre also has a section dedicated to the island's famous wine industry. Visitors can learn about the history of Madeira wine, see how it is produced, and even taste some of the different varieties.

Throughout the museum, visitors can enjoy stunning views of Funchal harbor and the surrounding mountains. There is also a gift shop where visitors can purchase souvenirs and locally-made crafts.

Overall, the Madeira Story Centre is a must-visit destination for anyone interested in learning about the history, culture, and natural wonders of Madeira. Its interactive exhibits and immersive displays make it a unique and memorable experience for visitors of all ages.

Frederico de Freitas Museum

The Frederico de Freitas Museum is a fascinating museum located in the heart of Funchal, Madeira. The museum is dedicated to showcasing the impressive collection of artifacts and antiques amassed by the museum's namesake, Dr. Frederico de Freitas.

Dr. Frederico de Freitas was a well-known Madeiran lawyer, politician, and collector who spent much of his life traveling the world and collecting rare and valuable objects. The museum is housed in Dr. de Freitas' former home, which he bequeathed to the municipality of Funchal upon his death in 1966.

The museum is divided into several themed sections, each showcasing a different aspect of Dr. de Freitas' extensive collection. Visitors can explore the different rooms of the house, each filled with unique and fascinating objects.

One of the most impressive sections of the museum is the one dedicated to furniture and interior design. Here, visitors can see beautifully crafted pieces from different time periods and styles, including Renaissance, Baroque, and Art Deco.

Another interesting section of the museum is the one dedicated to Portuguese ceramics. Visitors can see rare and unique pieces from different regions of Portugal, including azulejos (traditional blue and white tiles), faience (glazed earthenware), and porcelain.

The museum also features a section dedicated to jewelry and silverware, where visitors can see intricate pieces made by some of Portugal's most skilled craftsmen. Additionally, there is a section dedicated to paintings, where visitors can admire works by Portuguese artists as well as pieces from other countries.

Overall, the Frederico de Freitas Museum is a must-visit destination for anyone interested in art, history, and culture. The museum offers a unique glimpse into the life and collection of one of Madeira's most prominent citizens and is a testament to the island's rich cultural heritage.

Christopher Columbus House Museum

The Christopher Columbus House Museum is a fascinating museum located in the heart of Porto Santo, Madeira. The museum is dedicated to telling the story of Christopher Columbus' time on the island and his voyages of discovery to the New World.

The museum is housed in a beautiful 15th-century house where it is believed that Columbus lived during his time on the island. Visitors can explore the different rooms of the house, each filled with exhibits and displays that provide insights into Columbus' life and work.

One of the highlights of the museum is the collection of maps and navigational instruments from the Age of Discovery. Visitors can see how sailors like Columbus used these tools to navigate the world's oceans and make their way to new lands.

Another interesting exhibit in the museum is the section dedicated to Columbus' life on Porto Santo. Visitors can see recreations of the house where Columbus is believed to have lived, as well as exhibits on the island's history and culture.

The museum also features a section dedicated to Columbus' voyages of discovery. Visitors can learn about the different expeditions Columbus led and the impact they had on world history. There are also exhibits on the native cultures Columbus encountered on his journeys and the legacy of his voyages in the New World.

Overall, the Christopher Columbus House Museum offers a unique and immersive experience for visitors interested in the history of exploration and discovery. The museum's beautiful setting and extensive collection of artifacts and exhibits make it a place to be for anyone traveling to Porto Santo, Madeira.

São Vicente Caves and Volcanism Centre

The São Vicente Caves and Volcanism Centre is a remarkable geological attraction situated on the northern coast of Madeira Island. This unique complex offers visitors a chance to explore the island's volcanic origins and learn about its geological history in a hands-on and immersive way.

The caves are a series of volcanic tunnels formed over thousands of years by flowing lava. Visitors can explore these underground tunnels on a guided tour, marveling at the stunning geological formations, including lava stalactites and stalagmites, as well as the colorful mineral deposits that line the walls of the tunnels.

The Volcanism Centre, located adjacent to the caves, is an educational center that provides visitors with an in-depth understanding of the geological processes that have shaped Madeira Island. Here, visitors can learn about volcanic activity, earthquakes, and other natural phenomena that have affected the island over millions of years.

The center features interactive exhibits and displays that allow visitors to experience the power of a volcanic eruption, explore the different types of volcanic rocks, and learn about the plants and animals that have adapted to the island's unique geology.

One of the most impressive exhibits at the Volcanism Centre is the earthquake simulator, which gives visitors a sense of what it's like to experience a seismic event. Additionally, there is a section dedicated to the history of Madeira's volcanic activity, including information on the island's most recent volcanic eruption in 1957.

Overall, the São Vicente Caves and Volcanism Centre offers a fascinating and educational experience for visitors of all ages. Its unique geological formations, interactive exhibits, and stunning natural beauty make it a must-visit destination for anyone interested in learning about the island's volcanic origins and geological history.

Madeira Embroidery Museum

The Madeira Embroidery Museum is a charming museum located in the heart of Funchal, Madeira. The museum is dedicated to showcasing the unique and intricate embroidery work for which Madeira Island is renowned.

The museum features a collection of vintage and contemporary pieces, ranging from clothing and linens to tablecloths and decorative items. Visitors can marvel at the delicate embroidery stitches and intricate designs that have made Madeira embroidery a highly sought-after handicraft around the world.

One of the highlights of the museum is the embroidery workshops, where visitors can watch skilled artisans at work and even participate in a hands-on embroidery lesson. Visitors can learn about the different types of embroidery stitches used in Madeira embroidery and the traditional techniques that have been passed down via generations of artisans.

The museum also reveals a fascinating glimpse into the history of Madeira embroidery. Visitors can learn about the origins of the craft, which dates back to the 19th century when wealthy British and American tourists began commissioning local artisans to create embroidered items as souvenirs.

In addition to the exhibits on display, the museum also features a gift shop where visitors can purchase beautiful and unique Madeira embroidery items to take home as a souvenir.

Overall, the Madeira Embroidery Museum is a must-visit destination for anyone interested in the history and artistry of embroidery. Its collection of vintage and contemporary pieces, interactive workshops, and educational exhibits make it a fascinating and enriching experience for visitors of all ages.

Chapter 5

Top Attractions

Madeira is home to several fascinating attractions, from historical monuments and churches to modern-day amusement parks. From museums to outdoor activities, there are plenty of things to do in Madeira. Here are some of the top attractions in Madeira that you should visit on your next holiday.

Funchal, the capital city of Madeira, is a charming and vibrant destination that has something to offer for everyone. It is known for its colorful architecture, picturesque streets, and stunning natural beauty.

One of the most popular attractions in Funchal is the Old Town, or Zona Velha, which is a maze of narrow streets lined with charming old buildings painted in bright colors. The Old Town is a great place to wander around and explore, with its many restaurants, cafes, and shops. It is also home to the Mercado dos Lavradores, which is a must-visit for any foodie. Here you can find fresh fruits, vegetables, and seafood, as well as local specialties like Madeira wine, honey cake, and Poncha, a traditional drink made with aguardente, honey, and lemon.

Another must-visit attraction in Funchal is the Monte Palace Tropical Garden, which is located on a hill overlooking the city. The garden is home to a variety of exotic plants and flowers, as well as a collection of Asian art and artifacts. Visitors can take a cable car up to the garden, which offers stunning views of Funchal and the surrounding landscape.

For history lovers, Funchal has a rich cultural heritage that can be explored through its many museums and historic sites. The city's Cathedral, which dates back to the 15th century, is a must-visit for anyone interested in religious history. The Madeira Story Centre, located in the Old Town, is a great place to learn about the island's history, culture, and traditions. Another interesting museum is the Museum of Natural History, which showcases the unique flora and fauna of Madeira.

In addition to its cultural attractions, Funchal is also known for its beautiful beaches and outdoor activities. Praia Formosa is one of the most popular beaches in the city, with its clear waters and stunning views of the Atlantic Ocean. Visitors can also enjoy hiking in the nearby mountains, exploring the island's levadas, or taking a boat tour to see dolphins and whales in their natural habitat.

Food and drink are an essential part of the Madeiran experience, and Funchal has a thriving culinary scene that reflects the island's diverse cultural influences. The city is home to a wide range of restaurants, cafes, and bars, offering everything from traditional Madeiran dishes like Espetada and Bolo do Caco to international cuisine. Madeira wine, which is famous around the world for its unique flavor and aroma, is a must-try for any visitor to the island.

Funchal is a truly unique and unforgettable destination that offers something for everyone. Whether you are looking for history, culture, nature, or simply a relaxing getaway, Funchal has it all.

Monte Palace Tropical Garden

This is a popular tourist attraction in Funchal, the capital city of Madeira. Located on a hill overlooking the city, the garden is a beautiful and peaceful oasis that reveals beautiful views of the surrounding landscape.

The garden covers an area of around 70,000 square meters and is home to a wide variety of exotic plants and flowers from all over the world. Visitors can explore the garden's many winding paths, which lead through lush greenery, past waterfalls and ponds, and under arches of flowering vines.

One of the highlights of the garden is the collection of Asian art and artifacts, which is housed in the former Monte Palace Hotel. The collection includes a wide range of objects from China, Japan, and other parts of Asia, including porcelain, jade, and bronze sculptures, as well as paintings and textiles.

Another popular feature of the garden is the Crystal Palace, which is a replica of a Victorian-era glasshouse. The Crystal Palace houses a collection of tropical birds, including parrots and flamingos, and is a popular spot for visitors to take photos.

To reach the garden, visitors can take a cable car from Funchal up to the Monte neighborhood, which is located on the hill above the city. From there, it is a short walk to the entrance of the garden.

Overall, the Monte Palace Tropical Garden is a must-visit for anyone traveling to Madeira. Its stunning natural beauty, impressive collection of Asian art, and peaceful atmosphere make it a unique and unforgettable destination.

Levada Walks

Levada walks are a must-do experience for anyone visiting Madeira. These are unique trails that follow the ancient irrigation channels that have been used to bring water to the island's agricultural land for centuries. Not only are they a fascinating insight into Madeira's history and culture, but they also offer some of the most breathtaking views of the island's natural beauty.

There are over 2,000 kilometers of levadas in Madeira, but not all of them are suitable for hiking. The levada walks that are recommended for visitors are well-maintained and relatively easy to navigate, although some require a bit more physical effort than others.

One of the most popular levada walks is the Levada do Caldeirão Verde, which takes hikers through lush green forests and along steep cliff sides to a stunning waterfall. This walk is approximately 13 kilometers long and takes around 5-6 hours to complete. The path can be narrow and uneven in some parts, so it's important to wear appropriate footwear and take care.

Another popular levada walk is the Levada do Rei, which follows an easy, flat path through stunning scenery. This walk is approximately 10 kilometers long and takes around 3-4 hours to complete. Along the way, hikers will pass through tunnels and over aqueducts, and enjoy views of the island's rugged mountains and coastline.

For those who are looking for a more challenging levada walk, the Levada do Risco is a great option. This trail is approximately 7 kilometers long and takes around 3 hours to complete. The path is narrow and steep in some parts, but the stunning views of the valley and coastline make it all worthwhile.

It's important to note that levada walks can be affected by weather conditions, so it's always a good idea to check the forecast and trail conditions before setting out. It's also recommended to bring plenty of water and snacks, as well as a hat and sunscreen, as the sun can be strong in some parts of the island.

Overall, levada walks are an unforgettable experience that offer a unique glimpse into Madeira's natural beauty and rich history. Whether you're an experienced hiker or just looking for a leisurely stroll, there's a levada walk for everyone on this stunning island.

Cabo Girão cliff

If you're planning a trip to Madeira, Portugal, then Cabo Girão cliff is a must-visit destination. This stunning cliff is one of the highest sea cliffs in Europe and offers visitors a panoramic view of the Atlantic Ocean and Madeira's south coast. In this comprehensive guide, we will take a closer look at everything you need to know about Cabo Girão cliff, including how to get there, what to expect, and the best time to visit.

Cabo Girão is a cliff located on the south coast of Madeira, approximately 15 km from Funchal. It is a natural wonder that rises to a height of 580 meters above sea level. The cliff is known for its impressive glass platform, which extends over the cliff's edge and offers breathtaking views of the coastline below.

There are several ways to get to Cabo Girão cliff. The easiest and most convenient way is by car. You can rent a car from Funchal and take the highway towards Ribeira Brava. From there, you will need to follow the signs for Cabo Girão. Alternatively, you can take the bus from Funchal to Ribeira Brava and then catch another bus to Cabo Girão.

Cabo Girão cliff offers visitors an unforgettable experience. The glass platform provides a 360-degree view of the surrounding areas, including the Atlantic Ocean, Funchal, and the mountainous terrain. The platform is also a popular spot for photography enthusiasts, as it offers incredible photo opportunities.

Aside from the glass platform, there are several walking trails around the cliff that offer visitors a chance to explore the area further. The trails are well-marked and provide stunning views of the coastline.

When to visit Cabo Girão cliff is during the summer months, between June and September. During this time, the weather is warm and sunny, and there is less chance of rain. However, if you prefer a quieter experience, it's best to visit outside of the peak tourist season.

Tips for visiting

Wear comfortable shoes for walking on the trails

Bring a camera or smartphone for taking photos

Bring a jacket or sweater, as it can be windy at the top of the cliff

Avoid visiting during peak tourist season if you prefer a quieter experience

If you have a fear of heights, it's best to avoid the glass platform.

Cabo Girão cliff is a must-visit for visitors going to Madeira. Its impressive height and stunning views make it a popular spot for tourists and locals alike. Whether you're interested in photography, hiking, or simply taking in the natural beauty of the area, Cabo Girão cliff is an experience you won't forget. Just be sure to follow the tips above to make the most of your visit.

Pico do Arieiro mountain

Pico do Arieiro is a spectacular mountain in Madeira, Portugal, that offers breathtaking views of the island and beyond. As one of the highest peaks on Madeira, Pico do Arieiro is a must-visit destination for nature enthusiasts, hikers, and photographers. In this guide, we'll provide you with all the information you need to make the most of your visit to this stunning mountain.

There are several ways to get to Pico do Arieiro, depending on your preferences and budget. The easiest way is to rent a car and drive to the mountain. The road to Pico do Arieiro is well-maintained, although it can be narrow and winding in some sections. If you don't feel comfortable driving, you can also take a bus or join a guided tour.

Hiking Trails

Pico do Arieiro is famous for its hiking trails, which offer stunning views of the surrounding landscapes. The most popular trail is the Pico do Arieiro to Pico Ruivo hike, which takes about four hours to complete. The trail is well-marked and relatively easy, although it can be steep and narrow in some sections. Make sure to bring plenty of water, sunscreen, and a hat, as the sun can be intense on the mountain.

If you're looking for a more challenging hike, you can try the Pico do Arieiro to Achada do Teixeira trail, which takes about six hours to complete. This trail is less crowded than the Pico do Arieiro to Pico Ruivo trail and offers stunning views of the island's rugged landscapes.

Things to Do

Apart from hiking, there are several other things to do on Pico do Arieiro mountain. One of the most popular activities is stargazing, as the mountain offers a clear view of the night sky. You can also visit the Pico do Arieiro Observatory, which is located near the mountain's peak. The observatory offers guided tours and educational programs about astronomy and the universe.

If you're interested in the local flora and fauna, you can visit the nearby Ribeiro Frio Natural Park, which is home to various plant and animal species. The park offers different hiking trails, picnic areas, and stunning views of the island's landscapes.

The time to visit Pico do Arieiro is during the spring and summer months, when the weather is mild and sunny. The mountain can get quite chilly in the winter months, and there is a higher chance of rain and fog. Make sure to check the weather forecast before you plan your visit and bring appropriate clothing and gear.

Pico do Arieiro is a stunning mountain that offers a wide range of activities and experiences for visitors. Whether you're a hiker, photographer, or astronomy enthusiast, there's something for everyone on this beautiful peak. We hope this guide has provided you with all the information you need to plan your visit to Pico do Arieiro and make the most of your time on the mountain

Curral das Freiras valley

Curral das Freiras is a stunning valley nestled in the heart of Madeira, known for its dramatic landscapes and captivating beauty. Situated in the central mountain range of the island, this valley is a popular tourist destination on the island, attracting visitors from all over the world.

The name Curral das Freiras means "Nuns' Corral" in English, and it has an interesting history behind it. According to legend, a group of nuns sought refuge in this valley during a pirate attack on Funchal, the capital of Madeira, in the 16th century. The valley was so well hidden that the pirates never found them, and the nuns were able to escape unharmed. Today, the valley is a peaceful retreat that offers visitors a unique experience in the heart of Madeira.

One of the best ways to experience the beauty of Curral das Freiras is by taking a hike through the valley. There are several trails that wind through the valley, offering breathtaking views of the mountains and forests. One of the most popular trails is the Levada do Curral das Freiras, which follows an ancient irrigation channel through the valley. This trail is relatively easy and offers stunning views of the valley and the surrounding mountains.

Another popular activity in Curral das Freiras is visiting the local shops and restaurants. The valley is famous for its traditional cherry liqueur, Ginja de Curral das Freiras, which is made from the cherries that grow in the valley.

Visitors can sample this delicious liqueur at several local shops and restaurants, along with other local specialties such as honey cake and chestnut soup.

For those looking for a more adventurous experience, there are also several outdoor activities available in Curral das Freiras. The valley is a popular spot for paragliding, with several companies offering tandem flights that offer stunning views of the valley and the surrounding mountains. There are also several rock climbing routes in the area, offering a challenging experience for experienced climbers.

Overall, Curral das Freiras is a place to visit for anyone traveling to Madeira. With its stunning natural beauty, rich history, and unique cultural offerings, it is a place that will leave a lasting impression on visitors.

Porto Santo island

Porto Santo Island is a hidden gem of Madeira, located just a short ferry ride away from the main island. It is a small, rugged island that offers visitors a unique and authentic experience. With stunning beaches, breathtaking views, and a relaxed atmosphere, Porto Santo is the perfect place to escape the busyness of life.

Beaches

One of the main attractions of Porto Santo Island is its long, sandy beaches. The island boasts a 9-kilometer-long beach that stretches along the eastern coast. The beach is made up of fine, golden sand, which is said to have therapeutic properties due to its high concentration of magnesium. The sea is crystal clear, and the water is warm, making it perfect for swimming and other water activities. The beach is also ideal for sunbathing and taking long walks, as there is plenty of space for everyone.

Apart from enjoying the beach, visitors can also engage in a variety of activities on Porto Santo Island. One of the most popular activities is hiking, as the island has several well-marked trails that lead through stunning landscapes and offer breathtaking views. Visitors can also rent bikes or scooters and explore the island on their own. For those who enjoy water activities, there is windsurfing, snorkeling, and diving. Fishing is also a popular activity, as the island has a rich marine life.

Porto Santo Island has a rich history that dates back to the 15th century when it was discovered by Portuguese navigators. The island was an important stop for ships that sailed between Europe and Africa, and it played a key role in the colonization of Madeira. Visitors can learn about the island's history at the Casa Colombo Museum, which is located in the historic center of Vila Baleira, the island's main town. The museum has a collection of artifacts that tell the story of the island's past.

Porto Santo Island has a unique cuisine that is influenced by its history and location. Seafood is a staple of the island's cuisine, and visitors can enjoy fresh fish and shellfish at the island's many restaurants. The island also has its own wine, which is made from a grape variety that is unique to the island. Visitors can sample the wine at the various wineries on the island.

There are several accommodation options on Porto Santo Island, ranging from small guesthouses to luxury resorts. Most of the hotels and guesthouses are located in Vila Baleira, but there are also options in other parts of the island. Visitors can choose to stay in the town center, close to the beach, or in more remote areas for a more secluded experience.

Whale and dolphin watching

Whale and dolphin watching is an experience that you simply cannot miss during your visit to Madeira. This activity will give you the opportunity to observe these incredible marine creatures in their natural habitat, and it is an unforgettable experience that will stay with you forever.

Madeira is one of the best places in the world for whale and dolphin watching. The island is located in the Atlantic Ocean, and it is home to many different species of whales and dolphins. The waters around Madeira are deep and rich in nutrients, which attracts a wide variety of marine life.

When it comes to whale watching, the best time to visit Madeira is between April and October. During this period, the weather is usually warm and sunny, and the sea is calm. This makes it easy to spot whales and dolphins, as they come to the surface to breathe and play.

There are several different ways to experience whale and dolphin watching in Madeira. One option is to take a boat tour, which is the most popular choice for tourists. There are many tour operators on the island that offer whale and dolphin watching tours, and they provide a safe and comfortable environment for visitors.

During a boat tour, you will have the opportunity to see a wide variety of marine life, including different species of whales, dolphins, and even sea turtles. The tour guides are knowledgeable about the local wildlife, and they will provide you with interesting facts and information about the animals you see.

If you prefer a more adventurous experience, you can also go on a kayaking or stand-up paddleboarding tour. This allows you to get up close and personal with the whales and dolphins, and it is an exciting way to experience the beauty of the ocean.

Another option is to take a whale and dolphin watching tour on a catamaran. This provides a more luxurious experience, and it is a great choice for couples or families who want to enjoy a relaxing day on the water. The catamaran tours usually include food and drinks, and they provide a comfortable and spacious environment for passengers.

No matter which option you choose, it is important to remember that whale and dolphin watching should always be done responsibly. This means respecting the animals and their natural habitat, and following the guidelines and regulations set by the local authorities.

Whale and dolphin watching is a must-do activity during your visit to Madeira. It is an incredible experience that will allow you to see some of the most amazing creatures on the planet in their natural habitat.

Madeira Wine Cellars

Madeira wine cellars are a must-visit for any wine enthusiast or curious traveler visiting the Portuguese island of Madeira. The history and tradition of Madeira wine can be traced back to the 15th century when the Portuguese first began exploring and colonizing the island. Today, the Madeira wine cellars serve as a living testament to the rich and unique winemaking culture that has been cultivated on the island for centuries.

Located primarily in the city of Funchal, the Madeira wine cellars offer visitors the opportunity to learn about the winemaking process, sample different varieties of Madeira wine, and explore the history and culture of this special drink. The cellars are often housed in historic buildings, many of which have been in operation for generations and are still family-owned.

Visitors to the Madeira wine cellars can expect a unique and immersive experience, starting with a guided tour of the cellar itself. The tours typically cover the history of Madeira wine, the winemaking process, and the different types of grapes used in the production of the wine. The guides are often passionate and knowledgeable about Madeira wine, and are happy to answer any questions visitors may have.

After the tour, visitors are invited to sample different varieties of Madeira wine, ranging from dry to sweet and everything in between. Madeira wine is popular for its unique aging process, which involves heating the wine in barrels, a process called "estufagem." This results in a wine that is rich, complex, and full of flavor, with notes of caramel, nuts, and spices.

In addition to the traditional Madeira wine cellars, there are also a number of smaller, boutique wineries on the island that offer visitors a more intimate and personalized wine-tasting experience. These wineries often focus on producing small batches of high-quality wine, using traditional methods and locally sourced grapes.

Overall, the Madeira wine cellars offer visitors a unique and unforgettable experience, providing a glimpse into the history, culture, and traditions of this special island.

Chapter 6

Outdoor Activities

With its mild climate, Madeira is ideal for outdoor activities. From trekking in the rugged mountains to whale watching in the deep blue sea, Madeira offers a wide range of activities to choose from. Whether you're looking for an adrenaline rush or a leisurely sightseeing experience, there is something to suit every taste and budget. Read on to learn more about the many outdoor activities available in Madeira.

Hiking and Trekking

When it comes to hiking and trekking in Madeira, visitors are in for a treat. The island boasts an abundance of stunning landscapes, from rugged coastlines to verdant mountains, all waiting to be explored on foot. Whether you're a seasoned hiker or just starting out, there are plenty of trails to suit all abilities.

One of the most popular hiking destinations in Madeira is the Pico do Arieiro trail. This challenging trek takes you up to the island's third highest peak, offering breathtaking views along the way. The trail is well-marked, but it's important to come prepared with appropriate hiking gear, as the weather can be unpredictable and the terrain can be steep.

Another must-do hiking trail is the Levada do Caldeirão Verde. This beautiful route takes you along a levada (irrigation channel), through lush forests and past cascading waterfalls, until you reach the impressive Caldeirão Verde waterfall itself. The trail is moderately difficult and takes around 5 hours to complete, so be sure to bring plenty of water and snacks.

For those seeking a more challenging trek, the Pico Ruivo trail is a must. This trail takes you up to the highest peak on the island, offering stunning views of Madeira's rugged coastline and the surrounding mountains. The trail is steep and rocky in places, so it's important to wear sturdy hiking boots and take care on the more challenging sections.

If you're looking for a more leisurely hike, the Levada dos Tornos is a great option. This easy trail takes you through picturesque countryside, past charming villages and farms, and along a scenic levada. Along the way, you'll have plenty of opportunities to stop and take in the stunning scenery, and perhaps even sample some of the island's delicious local produce.

It's important to note that when hiking in Madeira, it's always a good idea to come prepared with appropriate gear, including sturdy hiking boots, a waterproof jacket, and plenty of water and snacks. The weather can change quickly, so it's also a good idea to check the forecast before setting out.

Overall, hiking and trekking in Madeira is an experience not to be missed. With a wide range of trails to suit all abilities, stunning scenery, and a unique island culture to discover along the way, it's no wonder that Madeira is becoming an increasingly popular destination for hikers and outdoor enthusiasts.

Mountain Biking

Mountain biking is a popular activity in Madeira, offering riders the chance to explore the island's rugged terrain and stunning landscapes on two wheels. With a variety of trails to suit all levels of experience, from beginners to seasoned riders, there's something for everyone in Madeira's mountain biking scene.

One of the most popular mountain biking destinations in Madeira is the area around Machico, on the east coast of the island. Here, riders can take on the challenging trails of the Ponta de São Lourenço nature reserve, with its rocky terrain and stunning coastal views. The trails in this area are best suited to experienced riders, as the terrain can be challenging in places.

For those seeking a more leisurely ride, the Levada do Norte trail is a great option. This scenic route takes you along a levada (irrigation channel), through lush forests and past charming villages, with plenty of opportunities to stop and take in the stunning scenery along the way. The trail is suitable for riders of all levels, but it's important to come prepared with appropriate gear, as the weather can be unpredictable.

Another popular mountain biking trail in Madeira is the Chão da Lagoa trail, which takes you through the heart of the island's mountainous interior. This challenging trail features steep ascents and descents, rocky terrain, and stunning views of the surrounding mountains. It's best suited to experienced riders, and it's important to come prepared with appropriate gear, including a helmet, gloves, and sturdy shoes.

When mountain biking in Madeira, it's important to be respectful of the environment and other trail users. Be sure to stick to designated trails, and avoid damaging fragile ecosystems or disturbing wildlife. It's also important to come prepared with plenty of water and snacks, as well as a map or GPS device to help navigate the trails.

Overall, mountain biking in Madeira is a thrilling and rewarding experience, offering riders the chance to explore the island's stunning scenery and challenging terrain on two wheels. With a variety of trails to suit all levels of experience, from leisurely rides to adrenaline-fueled descents, there's something for every rider in Madeira's mountain biking scene.

Canyoning

Canyoning is a thrilling adventure sport that is growing in popularity on the island of Madeira. This exciting activity involves exploring narrow canyons, gorges and waterfalls on foot, by rappelling down cliffs, sliding down natural water slides, and jumping into crystal clear pools of water below.

One of the best things about canyoning in Madeira is that it offers a unique perspective on the island's stunning landscapes. As you make your way down the canyon, you'll be surrounded by towering cliffs, lush vegetation, and the sound of rushing water echoing off the canyon walls. It's an experience that truly immerses you in the natural beauty of Madeira.

One of the most popular canyoning destinations in Madeira is Ribeiro Frio, located in the north of the island. Here, you'll find a series of narrow gorges and cascading waterfalls that are perfect for canyoning adventures. The area is also home to an abundance of flora and fauna, including endemic species such as the Madeira Laurel and the Trocaz Pigeon.

Another popular canyoning destination in Madeira is the Ribeira das Cales. This narrow canyon offers a challenging canyoning experience, with steep descents, tight passages, and adrenaline-fueled jumps into deep pools of water. It's an experience that is not for the faint of heart, but for those who are up for the challenge, it's an adventure that they will never forget.

When canyoning in Madeira, it's important to come prepared with appropriate gear, including a wetsuit, helmet, and sturdy footwear. It's also important to go with a reputable guide, who can help you navigate the canyon safely and ensure that you have the best possible experience.

Overall, canyoning in Madeira is an adventure sport that is not to be missed. It's a unique and thrilling way to enjoy the island's stunning landscapes and experience the natural beauty of Madeira in a truly unforgettable way.

Surfing and Bodyboarding

Surfing and bodyboarding are popular water sports in Madeira, attracting surfers and beach lovers from all over the world. With its crystal-clear waters, consistent waves, and stunning scenery, Madeira is the perfect destination for anyone looking to catch some waves or improve their surfing skills.

One of the best places to surf and bodyboard in Madeira is at Paul do Mar, a small fishing village on the island's south-west coast. Here, you'll find a range of waves to suit all levels of experience, from gentle breaks for beginners to powerful waves for more advanced surfers. The beach is also home to several surf schools, where visitors can take lessons and rent equipment.

Another popular surfing destination in Madeira is Jardim do Mar, a charming village famous for its consistent waves and laid-back vibe. The beach here is less crowded than some of the other surfing spots on the island, making it a great place to escape the crowds and enjoy some quality surfing time. The area is also home to several surf shops and schools, where visitors can rent equipment.

For bodyboarders, Praia da Fajã da Areia is one of the best places to catch some waves in Madeira. Located on the north coast of the island, this secluded beach offers a range of waves to suit all levels of experience, from gentle swells to more challenging breaks. The beach is also home to several local bodyboarding clubs, where visitors can meet like-minded enthusiasts and learn more about the sport.

When surfing or bodyboarding in Madeira, it's important to come prepared with appropriate gear, including a wetsuit, leash, and surfboard or bodyboard. It's also important to check the weather and surf conditions before heading out, as conditions can change quickly and unexpectedly.

Overall, surfing and bodyboarding in Madeira are exciting and rewarding experiences, offering visitors the chance to explore the island's stunning coastline and catch some waves in one of the most beautiful and unique surfing destinations in the world.

Scuba Diving and Snorkeling

Scuba diving and snorkeling are popular activities in Madeira, offering visitors the opportunity to explore the island's stunning marine life and crystal-clear waters. With its warm temperatures, excellent visibility, and diverse marine ecosystem, Madeira is a great place to discover the underwater world.

One of the best places to go scuba diving in Madeira is at Garajau Marine Reserve, located on the south coast of the island. This protected area is home to a variety of marine species, including barracudas, octopuses, and rays, and features underwater caves and rock formations. The reserve is also home to a statue of Christ, which can be viewed underwater and is a popular attraction for divers.

For snorkelers, the natural pools of Porto Moniz are a place to be. These volcanic pools offer crystal-clear waters and a range of marine life, including colorful fish and sea urchins. The pools are also surrounded by stunning natural scenery, with towering cliffs and lush vegetation.

Another popular scuba diving destination in Madeira is the wreck of the Bowbelle, a cargo ship that sank off the coast of Madeira in 1995. The wreck is now a popular diving site, attracting divers from all over the world who come to explore the ship's rusting hull and discover the marine life that has made it its home.

When scuba diving or snorkeling in Madeira, it's important to go with a reputable guide or dive center, who can provide you with the necessary equipment and ensure that you have a safe and enjoyable experience. It's also important to respect the marine environment and follow responsible diving practices to help protect the delicate ecosystem.

Overall, scuba diving and snorkeling in Madeira offer visitors the chance to discover a world of underwater beauty and explore the island's stunning marine ecosystem. It's an experience that is not to be missed for anyone looking to discover the natural wonders of Madeira.

Paragliding and Hang Gliding

These are exhilarating activities that allow visitors to experience the beauty of Madeira from a unique perspective. With its stunning coastal cliffs and rugged mountain ranges, Madeira offers some of the best paragliding and hang gliding spots in the world.

One of the best places to go paragliding in Madeira is from Pico do Arieiro, the third highest peak on the island. From here, you can soar high above the mountains and enjoy breathtaking views of the island's dramatic scenery. The landing spot is located in Funchal, the island's capital, which means you'll be able to see the city from a whole new angle.

For hang gliders, the Ponta do Pargo cliff is a popular launching point, offering panoramic views of the Atlantic Ocean and the island's coastline. The cliff is located on the westernmost point of the island and is known for its challenging wind conditions, making it a great spot for experienced hang gliders looking for a thrill.

When paragliding or hang gliding in Madeira, it's important to go with a reputable guide or tour company, who can provide you with the necessary equipment and ensure that you have a safe and enjoyable experience. It's also important to check out the weather conditions and to avoid flying in strong winds or during stormy weather.

Overall, paragliding and hang gliding in Madeira offer visitors a thrilling and unforgettable way to experience the island's natural beauty. Whether you're an experienced flier or a first-time adventurer, you're sure to have a memorable experience soaring above the stunning landscape of Madeira.

Fishing and Sailing

Fishing and sailing are popular activities in Madeira, offering visitors the chance to experience the island's stunning coastline and rich marine life. With its warm waters and diverse ecosystem, Madeira is a great place to try your hand at fishing or take a leisurely sail along the coast.

For fishing enthusiasts, Madeira offers a variety of options, from deep-sea fishing to shore fishing. The waters around the island are home to a range of fish species, including tuna, marlin, swordfish, and barracuda. Many fishing charters and tours are available to take visitors out to sea, with experienced guides who can help you find the best fishing spots and provide you with the necessary equipment.

For those looking for a more leisurely way to enjoy the ocean, sailing is a great option. The calm waters around Madeira's coastline offer a peaceful and relaxing sailing experience, with stunning views of the island's rugged cliffs and rocky shores. Many sailing tours and charters are available, offering visitors the chance to explore the island's coastline and discover hidden coves and beaches.

In addition to fishing and sailing, Madeira also hosts an annual regatta, the Madeira Island Ultra-Trail, which attracts sailors and runners from all over the world. This challenging event takes participants on a scenic route around the island, showcasing the beauty of Madeira's coastline and mountainous terrain.

When fishing or sailing in Madeira, it's important to follow responsible practices to help protect the marine environment. This includes using sustainable fishing methods and avoiding areas where marine life is known to be at risk. It's also important to respect the ocean and its inhabitants, taking care not to disturb or damage the delicate ecosystem.

Overall, fishing and sailing in Madeira offer visitors a unique and memorable way to experience the island's natural beauty and rich marine life. Whether you're a fishing enthusiast or a leisurely sailor, you're sure to enjoy the stunning views and peaceful atmosphere of the island's coastline.

Golfing

Golfing is a popular activity in Madeira, offering visitors the chance to enjoy the island's stunning landscapes while playing on some of the world's most beautiful courses. With its mild climate and diverse terrain, Madeira is a great place to play golf year-round, making it a top destination for golfers from around the world.

One of the most famous golf courses in Madeira is the Santo da Serra Golf Club, located in the hills above the city of Funchal. This challenging course offers views of the Atlantic Ocean and the surrounding mountains, with a range of obstacles and hazards to test even the most skilled golfers.

Another popular golf course is the Palheiro Golf Club, situated on the outskirts of Funchal. This 18-hole course is set amid the island's lush vegetation and offers panoramic views of the sea and the city. The course also features a clubhouse with a restaurant and bar, where golfers can relax and enjoy the stunning views after their game.

In addition to these courses, Madeira also hosts a number of golfing events throughout the year, including the Madeira Island Open, which attracts some of the world's top golfers. The event is held at different courses each year, providing golfers with the chance to play on a variety of stunning courses across the island.

Whether you're a seasoned golfer or a beginner, Madeira's golf courses offer a unique and unforgettable golfing experience. With its stunning landscapes and mild climate, Madeira is the perfect destination for a golfing holiday, where you can enjoy the game in a beautiful and relaxing environment.

Chapter 7

Food and Drink

Madeira is a beautiful island with a long-standing history of producing delicious food and drink. It has been a major source of inspiration for Portuguese cooking for centuries, and its unique ingredients, flavors, and cooking techniques have been adopted by cooks across the world. The island's cuisine is known for its seafood, tropical fruits, and spices, as well as its famous Madeira wines.

Madeira's local drinks, such as poncha, are also popular and can be found in many bars and restaurants around the island. Whether you're looking for a traditional meal or something more exotic, there's something for everyone in Madeira's food and drink scene.

Typical Dishes and Ingredients

Visitors to the island are in for a treat when it comes to food, as Madeira boasts a unique blend of traditional Portuguese dishes, as well as its own local specialties. In this guide, we'll delve into some of the typical dishes and ingredients you can expect to find when dining in Madeira.

One of the most iconic dishes in Madeira is "espetada," which consists of chunks of beef, marinated with garlic, bay leaves, and salt, skewered onto a bay leaf stick, and then grilled over hot coals. This dish is typically served with baked sweet potatoes and salad. Another popular dish is "bolo do caco," a type of bread made with sweet potato, which is served warm and topped with garlic butter or cheese.

Seafood is also a significant part of the Madeiran diet. Visitors can try "espada com banana," which is a dish consisting of swordfish, served with banana and local sweet potato. Other seafood dishes to try include "caldeirada," a fish stew made with a variety of local fish and vegetables, and "lapas grelhadas," grilled limpets that are a local delicacy.

Meat lovers will enjoy "cozido," a meat and vegetable stew that is slow-cooked for hours, as well as "carne vinho e alhos," a dish of marinated pork that is typically served with rice and beans. "Sopa de tomate," a tomato-based soup with bread, herbs, and poached eggs, is another local specialty.

For those with a sweet tooth, Madeira has plenty of desserts to offer. "Bolo de mel," a honey cake that is made with local sugar cane molasses, is a must-try. Other popular desserts include "queijadas," small cheesecakes made with cottage cheese and sugar, and "pudim de maracujá," a passionfruit custard that is light and refreshing.

In terms of ingredients, Madeira is famous for its wine, which is produced on the island using traditional methods.

Visitors can try a glass of the famous Madeira wine, which is sweet and fortified. The island is also known for its local honey, sugar cane molasses, and fresh fruits and vegetables, which are used in many dishes.

Madeira's cuisine is a unique blend of traditional Portuguese dishes and local specialties that reflect the island's rich history and culture. From "espetada" to "bolo do caco" to "bolo de mel," there is no shortage of delicious and unique dishes to try. Visitors to Madeira are in for a treat when it comes to food, and we hope this guide has provided some insight into the typical dishes and ingredients you can expect to find on the island.

Best Restaurants and Bars

Madeira is home to a diverse culinary scene, with plenty of restaurants and bars offering a range of local and international cuisine. Here are some of the best places to eat and drink on the island:

Restaurante Il Gallo D'Oro: This Michelin-starred restaurant is located in the luxury hotel The Cliff Bay and offers a refined dining experience with a focus on local ingredients and flavors.

Restaurante Do Forte: Set in a historic fortress overlooking the sea, this restaurant serves fresh seafood dishes and traditional Madeiran cuisine.

O Jango: A popular spot among locals, O Jango offers a relaxed atmosphere and delicious meat and fish dishes, including the iconic espetada.

Taberna Ruel: This cozy bar and restaurant in Funchal's old town serves a range of tapas-style dishes and traditional Madeiran fare, as well as local wines and cocktails.

William Restaurant: Set in a beautifully restored 18th-century mansion, William Restaurant offers contemporary cuisine with a focus on local ingredients and flavors.

Poncha da Serra: This traditional bar in Camara de Lobos is known for its namesake drink, poncha, a local specialty made with aguardente (a type of brandy), honey, and citrus juice.

The Wine Lodge: Located in Funchal's historic center, The Wine Lodge offers a wide selection of Madeira wines, as well as tapas-style dishes and live music.

Armazém do Sal: This trendy restaurant and bar in the old town of Funchal serves modern European cuisine and creative cocktails in a stylish setting.

Beerhouse: With over 100 beers on offer, Beerhouse is a must-visit spot for beer lovers. The bar also serves delicious snacks and tapas-style dishes.

Madeira Rum House: This atmospheric bar in the heart of Funchal's old town offers a range of local rums and cocktails, as well as live music and a cozy ambiance.

Madeira offers a diverse range of dining and drinking options, from Michelin-starred restaurants to cozy local bars.

Farmers' Markets and Food Festivals

For foodies visiting Madeira, the island offers a range of farmers' markets and food festivals where you can sample some of the freshest local produce and traditional dishes. Here are some of the best places to visit:

Mercado dos Lavradores: Located in the heart of Funchal, this colorful market is a must-visit for anyone interested in local produce. Here you can find fresh fruits and vegetables, flowers, and traditional Madeiran delicacies such as honey cake and bolo do caco.

Mercado da Penteada: This indoor market in Funchal offers a range of fresh produce, including fruit, vegetables, and local cheeses and meats.

Santana Farmers' Market: Held every Sunday in the picturesque town of Santana, this market offers a range of local produce and traditional crafts.

Ribeira Brava Farmers' Market: This market in the town of Ribeira Brava is held every Sunday and offers a range of fresh produce, including fruits and vegetables, honey, and homemade jams.

Madeira Wine Festival: Held every September, the Madeira Wine Festival celebrates the island's famous fortified wine with tastings, live music, and a parade of traditional Madeiran costumes.

Santo da Serra Apple Festival: Held every October in the town of Santo da Serra, this festival celebrates the local apple harvest with food stalls, live music, and a traditional apple market.

Madeira Gastronomy Festival: Held every November, the Madeira Gastronomy Festival showcases the island's culinary heritage with a range of food-related events, including cooking classes, tastings, and traditional Madeiran banquets.

Madeira offers plenty of opportunities for foodies to sample local produce and traditional dishes at farmers' markets and food festivals throughout the year. Whether you're looking for fresh fruits and vegetables, traditional Madeiran delicacies, or a glass of the island's famous wine, you're sure to find something to delight your taste buds on this beautiful island.

Wine Production and Tastings

Madeira is famous for its unique fortified wine, which has been produced on the island since the 16th century. Here's what you need to know about Madeira wine production and tastings:

Madeira wine is made by adding neutral grape spirit to fermenting grape juice. This process stops the fermentation and creates a sweet, fortified wine that can be aged for decades or even centuries.

There are four main grape varieties used in Madeira wine production: Sercial, Verdelho, Bual, and Malmsey. Each grape variety produces a different style of wine, ranging from dry to sweet.

The wine is aged in barrels in warm environments, which accelerates the aging process and creates unique flavors and aromas. The wine is often aged for many years or even decades before it is bottled and sold.

There are several wineries on Madeira that offer tours and tastings, including Blandy's, Henriques & Henriques, and Barbeito. Visitors can learn about the wine production process, sample different styles of Madeira wine, and purchase bottles to take home.

Madeira wine tastings often include a range of vintages and styles, including dry and sweet wines. Tastings may also include food pairings, such as cheese or chocolate, to complement the flavors of the wine.

Madeira wine is also used in cooking, particularly in sauces and desserts. The wine's unique flavor and sweetness make it a popular ingredient in traditional Madeiran dishes such as bolo de mel (honey cake) and espada com banana (scabbard fish with banana).

Madeira wine production is a unique process that results in a one-of-a-kind fortified wine with complex flavors and aromas. Visitors to the island can learn about the wine production process and sample different styles of Madeira wine at local wineries, as well as enjoy the wine in traditional Madeiran dishes.

Chapter 8

Practical Information

As you prepare for your journey to this stunning Portuguese archipelago, it's essential to equip yourself with practical information that will make your trip enjoyable and memorable. From the island's rich cultural heritage to its awe-inspiring natural landscapes, Madeira is a destination that promises to delight visitors from all walks of life. Let's dive into the practical information you need to know for your Madeira adventure.

Health and Safety Tips

As a popular tourist destination, Madeira boasts of numerous attractions ranging from stunning beaches to magnificent natural landscapes. However, it is essential to prioritize health and safety when visiting the island to ensure a pleasant and unforgettable experience.

Here are some health and safety tips to help visitors stay safe and healthy during their trip to Madeira:

Vaccinations: It is crucial to check with your healthcare provider about any required or recommended vaccinations for Madeira. Vaccinations such as tetanus, hepatitis A, and typhoid are commonly recommended for travelers.

Sun Protection: Madeira is blessed with a sunny climate, which makes it essential to wear sun-protective clothing, sunglasses, and hats to protect yourself from sunburn and skin damage. Applying sunscreen with a high SPF is also crucial, especially during the hottest hours of the day.

Stay Hydrated: The warm weather in Madeira can cause dehydration, making it necessary to carry enough drinking water and other hydrating beverages, especially when out and about exploring the island.

Food and Drink: Madeira is known for its delicious food, but visitors should be cautious when trying new dishes. Only eat food from reputable restaurants, and avoid consuming undercooked meats, raw seafood, or tap water. Instead, opt for bottled water, and ensure that any fruits and vegetables have been properly washed and peeled before consumption.

First Aid Kit: Carrying a first aid kit with basic medication such as painkillers, antihistamines, and plasters can help in case of minor injuries or allergies.

Road Safety: Visitors planning on renting a car should be familiar with the rules of the road in Madeira. Drive on the right-hand side of the road, adhere to speed limits, and avoid driving after drinking alcohol. Also, it is essential to note that some roads in Madeira can be narrow and winding, making it necessary to exercise caution while driving.

Emergency Contacts: Always have emergency contacts, including the local police, hospital, and embassy or consulate, on hand in case of any unforeseen events or emergencies.

Madeira is an exceptional travel destination with numerous attractions, but visitors should prioritize their health and safety during their stay. By adhering to the above health and safety tips, visitors can have a safe and memorable trip to Madeira.

Emergency Contacts

Madeira is a beautiful island paradise, but like any destination, it is important for visitors to be prepared for any unforeseen emergencies. Whether you are traveling solo or with a group, it is crucial to have a list of emergency contacts readily available to you. In this guide, we will provide you with an overview of important emergency contacts to keep in mind when visiting Madeira.

Emergency Services: In the event of an emergency, the first number to call is 112. This is the national emergency number in Portugal and is used for all emergency services, including ambulance, fire, and police services. The service is available 24/7 and the call is free of charge.

Hospitals and Medical Centers: If you need medical attention, there are several hospitals and medical centers available throughout Madeira. Some of the major hospitals in Madeira include Hospital Dr. Nélio Mendonça, Hospital dos Marmeleiros, and Hospital Particular da Madeira. All of these hospitals have emergency services available 24/7.

Pharmacies: Pharmacies in Madeira are typically open from 9 am to 1 pm and from 3 pm to 7 pm on weekdays, and from 9 am to 1 pm on Saturdays. If you need to find a pharmacy outside of these hours, you can call the Pharmacy Association of Madeira on +351 291 228 825 for information on emergency pharmacies.

Embassies and Consulates: If you are a foreign national visiting Madeira, it is a good idea to know the location of your embassy or consulate. In the event that you lose your passport or need assistance from your home country, your embassy or consulate can provide you with the necessary support. Some of the major embassies and consulates in Madeira include the British Consulate, the Canadian Consulate, and the U.S. Consulate.

Transportation: If you are involved in a car accident or require assistance while driving, you can call the Madeira Regional Civil Protection Service on +351 291 700 112. If you need to report a theft or lost property on public transportation, you can call the Public Transportation Security Division on +351 291 208 000.

Natural Disasters: Madeira is prone to natural disasters such as earthquakes, landslides, and forest fires. In the event of a natural disaster, it is important to follow the instructions of local authorities and stay up to date with the latest news and information. The Madeira Civil Protection Service provides information on natural disasters and how to stay safe during an emergency.

It is always better to be safe than sorry when it comes to traveling. Having a list of emergency contacts readily available can make all the difference in the event of an emergency. Make sure to keep this guide handy during your trip to Madeira and enjoy your stay on this beautiful island.

Internet and Phone Services

When it comes to traveling to Madeira, visitors need to know that they can easily stay connected with the world through various internet and phone services available on the island. To make their stay comfortable, visitors must have access to internet and phone services. In this guide, we will discuss the various options available for visitors to stay connected while on the island.

Internet Services

One of the best ways to stay connected while on Madeira is through the internet. Visitors can access the internet through Wi-Fi, mobile data, or internet cafes. Here are some details about each option:

Wi-Fi: Most hotels, cafes, and restaurants on Madeira offer free Wi-Fi to their customers. Visitors can easily access the internet by asking for the Wi-Fi password. It is important to note that the quality of the internet connection can vary, depending on the location and the number of users connected to the same network.

Mobile Data: Visitors can also use mobile data services to access the internet. There are three main mobile network operators in Madeira, namely MEO, Vodafone, and NOS. Visitors can purchase SIM cards from any of these operators and use them to access the internet. However, it is important to check the coverage of the network operator before purchasing a SIM card.

Internet Cafes: Visitors can also use internet cafes to access the internet. There are many internet cafes located in the main cities of Madeira, and they offer high-speed internet services at an affordable price.

Phone Services

Visitors can also stay connected through phone services while on Madeira. Visitors can make calls, send texts, and access the internet through their phones. Here are some details about the phone services available:

Mobile Phones: Visitors can use their mobile phones to make calls and send texts while on Madeira. However, it is important to note that roaming charges may apply, and visitors should check with their mobile network operator before traveling to Madeira.

Local SIM Cards: Visitors can also purchase local SIM cards from any of the three main mobile network operators in Madeira, namely MEO, Vodafone, and NOS. These SIM cards offer affordable rates for local calls and texts.

Public Phones: There are also public phones available on Madeira, where visitors can make calls using coins or prepaid cards. These phones are usually located in busy areas such as airports, train stations, and bus terminals.

Visitors to Madeira have various options available for internet and phone services, which include Wi-Fi, mobile data, internet cafes, mobile phones, local SIM cards, and public phones.

Shopping and Souvenirs

When traveling to Madeira, visitors can look forward to a shopping experience unlike any other. From charming boutiques to bustling markets, Madeira offers a diverse range of shopping options to cater to all tastes and budgets.

Souvenirs are a popular choice for travelers, and Madeira has an abundance of options to choose from. One of the most iconic souvenirs is the Madeira wine, which is produced from grapes grown on the island. Visitors can purchase bottles of this sweet fortified wine at local wineries or wine shops, and even take a tour of the production facilities to learn more about the winemaking process.

For those looking for a more unique souvenir, the traditional embroidery of Madeira is a must-see. This delicate needlework is known for its intricate designs and vibrant colors, and can be found on everything from tablecloths to clothing. Visitors can visit the embroidery factories in Funchal, the capital city, to see the embroidery being made and purchase their own piece to take home.

Another popular souvenir is the wickerwork of Madeira, which is crafted from the branches of the willow tree. The skilled artisans of Madeira have been creating these intricate baskets and other items for centuries, and visitors can purchase them at markets and shops throughout the island.

In addition to souvenirs, visitors to Madeira will also find a wide variety of shopping opportunities for everyday items. Funchal boasts several shopping centers and malls, where visitors can find international brands and designer goods. For a more authentic shopping experience, visitors can head to the local markets, such as the Mercado dos

Lavradores, where they can browse fresh produce, seafood, and other local goods.

Overall, shopping in Madeira offers a unique opportunity to discover the island's local culture and traditions through its handicrafts and food products. Visitors are sure to find the perfect souvenir to remember their trip and bring a piece of Madeira home with them.

Tipping and Etiquette

Tipping and etiquette are important aspects of any culture and can vary widely from one country to another. Madeira, a stunning archipelago located off the coast of Portugal in the Atlantic Ocean, has its own unique customs and traditions when it comes to tipping and etiquette. In this travel guide, we will explore everything visitors need to know about tipping and etiquette in Madeira.

Tipping in Madeira

Tipping in Madeira is not mandatory, but it is appreciated for good service. The amount of the tip depends on the type of service provided, but a good rule of thumb is to tip between 5% and 10% of the total bill. For example, if you go to a restaurant and have a bill of €50, a tip of €2.50 to €5 would be appropriate.

It is important to note that some restaurants in Madeira include a service charge on the bill, so it is always a good idea to check the bill before you leave a tip. If a service charge is included, you may still want to leave a small additional tip for exceptional service.

Tipping in hotels in Madeira is also not mandatory, but it is appreciated. The amount of the tip depends on the level of service provided. For example, if you receive exceptional service from a hotel staff member, you may want to leave a tip of €5 to €10.

In taxis, tipping is not expected, but rounding up the fare to the nearest euro is common practice. For example, if the fare is €7.50, rounding up to €8 would be a polite gesture.

Etiquette in Madeira

Like any culture, Madeira has its own unique set of customs and traditions that visitors should be aware of. Here are a few examples:

Greetings: When meeting someone in Madeira, it is customary to greet them with a handshake or a kiss on both cheeks. This is true for both men and women. It is also polite to address people by their formal titles, such as "Senhor" or "Senhora," followed by their last name.

Dress code: Madeira has a warm climate, so light, comfortable clothing is recommended. However, it is important to dress appropriately when visiting religious sites or attending formal events. Shorts and sleeveless tops may not be permitted in certain places, so it is always a good idea to check beforehand.

Table manners: When dining in Madeira, it is polite to wait for the host to start eating before beginning your own meal. It is also customary to keep your hands visible on the table and to use utensils to eat, rather than your hands. Finally, it is considered impolite to leave food on your plate, so it is a good idea to only take what you can eat.

Respect for the elderly: In Madeira, there is a strong tradition of respecting and caring for the elderly. It is common to see younger people giving up their seats on public transportation or helping the elderly with their bags. Visitors to Madeira should also show respect to the elderly by addressing them with formal titles and using polite language.

Understanding the customs and traditions of Madeira when it comes to tipping and etiquette is an important part of being a respectful and courteous visitor. By following these guidelines, visitors can show their appreciation for the local culture and make their trip to Madeira an enjoyable and memorable experience.

Conclusion

Madeira is a destination that should not be missed by any traveler. Its stunning natural beauty, rich history, and unique culture make it a truly unforgettable place to visit. Whether you're looking to relax on the beach, explore historic sites, or indulge in delicious local cuisine, Madeira has something for everyone.

As we have explored in this travel guide, there are countless attractions and activities to enjoy in Madeira. From hiking the beautiful levadas to sampling the famous Madeira wine, visitors are sure to find an experience that suits their interests.

However, it is important to remember that visiting Madeira also comes with certain responsibilities. As a visitor to this beautiful island, it is important to show respect for the local culture and customs, including tipping and etiquette practices. By doing so, visitors can ensure that they are making a positive impact on the local community and contributing to the preservation of this unique destination for generations to come.

Madeira is a destination that offers much more than just beautiful beaches and scenery. It is a place that is rich in history, culture, and tradition, and a visit to this magical island is sure to be an experience that will stay with you for a lifetime.

Travel Planner

TRAVEL

DATE:

DURATION:

DESTINATION:

PLACES TO SEE:	LOCAL FOOD TO TRY:
1	1
2	2
3	3
4	4
5	5
6	6
7	7

DAY 1	DAY 2	DAY 3

DAY 4	DAY 5	DAY 6

NOTES	EXPENSES IN TOTAL:

PLANNER

TRAVEL

DATE:

DURATION:

DESTINATION:

PLACES TO SEE:	LOCAL FOOD TO TRY:
1	1
2	2
3	3
4	4
5	5
6	6
7	7

DAY 1	DAY 2	DAY 3

DAY 4	DAY 5	DAY 6

NOTES	EXPENSES IN TOTAL:

PLANNER

TRAVEL

DATE:

DURATION:

DESTINATION:

PLACES TO SEE:	LOCAL FOOD TO TRY:
1	1
2	2
3	3
4	4
5	5
6	6
7	7

DAY 1	DAY 2	DAY 3

DAY 4	DAY 5	DAY 6

NOTES	EXPENSES IN TOTAL:

PLANNER

TRAVEL

DATE:

DURATION:

DESTINATION:

PLACES TO SEE:	LOCAL FOOD TO TRY:
1	1
2	2
3	3
4	4
5	5
6	6
7	7

DAY 1	DAY 2	DAY 3

DAY 4	DAY 5	DAY 6

NOTES	EXPENSES IN TOTAL:

PLANNER

TRAVEL

DATE:

DURATION:

DESTINATION:

PLACES TO SEE:

1
2
3
4
5
6
7

LOCAL FOOD TO TRY:

1
2
3
4
5
6
7

DAY 1	DAY 2	DAY 3

DAY 4	DAY 5	DAY 6

NOTES	EXPENSES IN TOTAL:

PLANNER

TRAVEL

DATE:

DURATION:

DESTINATION:

PLACES TO SEE:	LOCAL FOOD TO TRY:
1 _____	1 _____
2 _____	2 _____
3 _____	3 _____
4 _____	4 _____
5 _____	5 _____
6 _____	6 _____
7 _____	7 _____

DAY 1	DAY 2	DAY 3

DAY 4	DAY 5	DAY 6

NOTES	EXPENSES IN TOTAL:

PLANNER

TRAVEL

DATE:

DURATION:

DESTINATION:

PLACES TO SEE:	LOCAL FOOD TO TRY:
1	1
2	2
3	3
4	4
5	5
6	6
7	7

DAY 1	DAY 2	DAY 3

DAY 4	DAY 5	DAY 6

NOTES	EXPENSES IN TOTAL:

PLANNER

TRAVEL

DATE:

DURATION:

DESTINATION:

PLACES TO SEE:	LOCAL FOOD TO TRY:
1	1
2	2
3	3
4	4
5	5
6	6
7	7

DAY 1	DAY 2	DAY 3

DAY 4	DAY 5	DAY 6

NOTES	EXPENSES IN TOTAL:

PLANNER

TRAVEL

DATE:

DURATION:

DESTINATION:

PLACES TO SEE:	LOCAL FOOD TO TRY:
1	1
2	2
3	3
4	4
5	5
6	6
7	7

DAY 1	DAY 2	DAY 3

DAY 4	DAY 5	DAY 6

NOTES	EXPENSES IN TOTAL:

PLANNER

TRAVEL

DATE:

DURATION:

DESTINATION:

PLACES TO SEE:	LOCAL FOOD TO TRY:
1	1
2	2
3	3
4	4
5	5
6	6
7	7

DAY 1	DAY 2	DAY 3

DAY 4	DAY 5	DAY 6

NOTES	EXPENSES IN TOTAL:

PLANNER

TRAVEL

DATE:

DURATION:

DESTINATION:

PLACES TO SEE:	LOCAL FOOD TO TRY:
1	1
2	2
3	3
4	4
5	5
6	6
7	7

DAY 1	DAY 2	DAY 3

DAY 4	DAY 5	DAY 6

NOTES	EXPENSES IN TOTAL:

PLANNER

Printed in Great Britain
by Amazon

24010521R00079